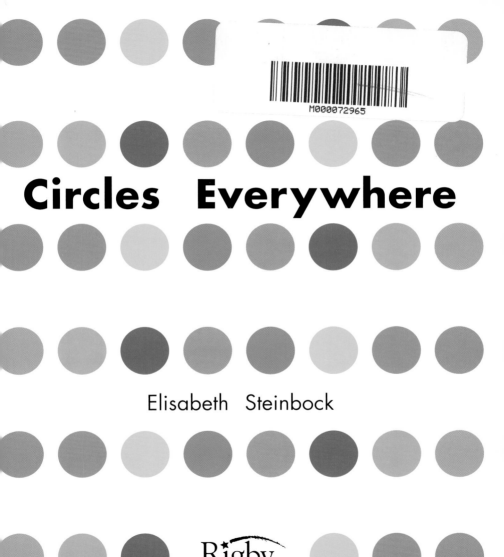

Circles Everywhere

Elisabeth Steinbock

Rigby

The clock is a circle.

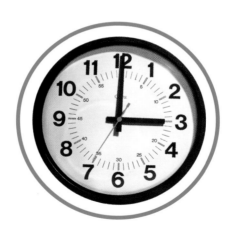

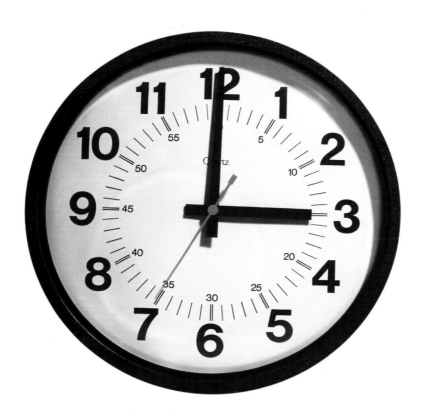

3

The table is a circle.

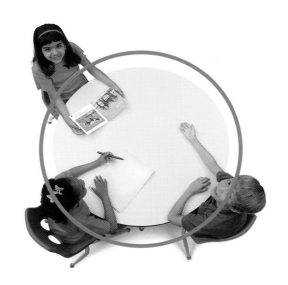

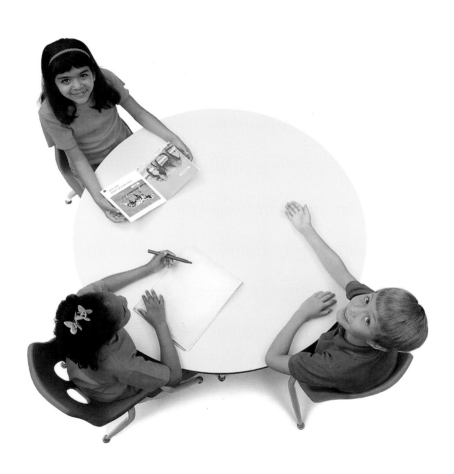

The plate is a circle.

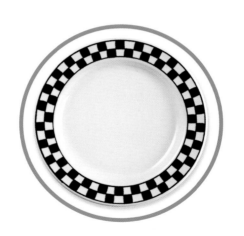

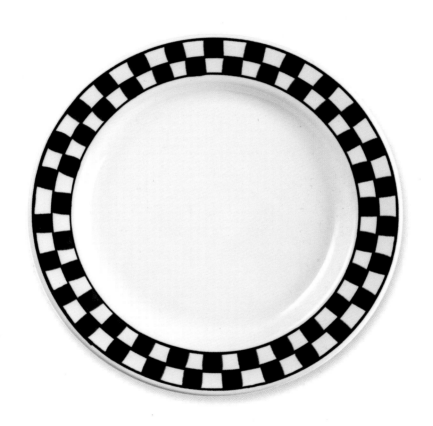

The sign is a circle.

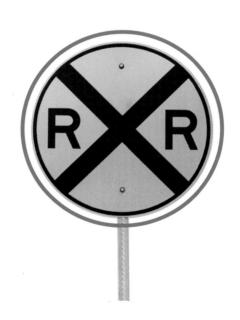

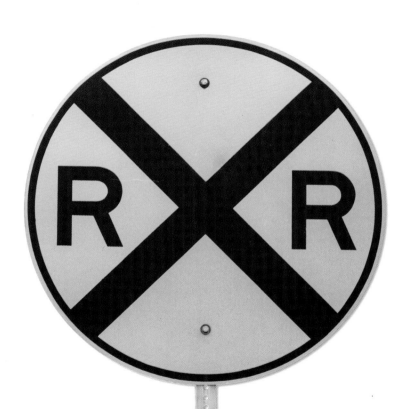

The cookie is a circle.

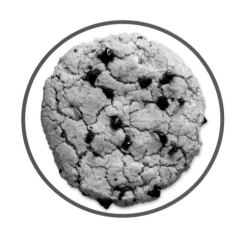

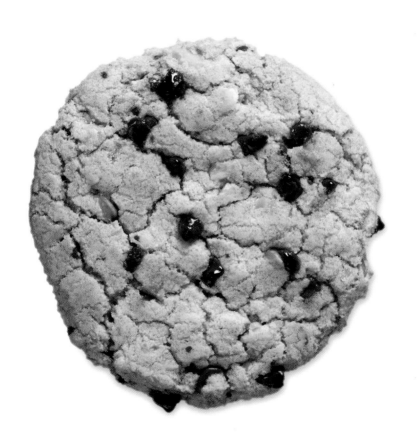

The ring is a circle.

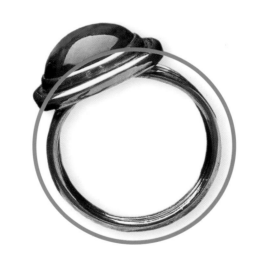

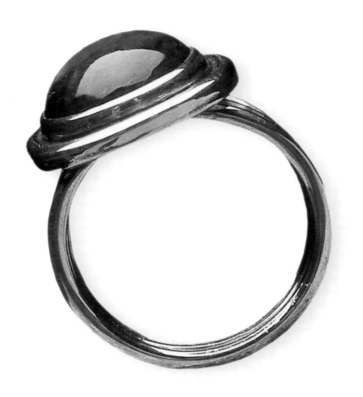

13

The ball is a circle.

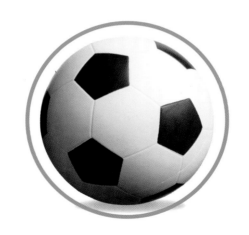

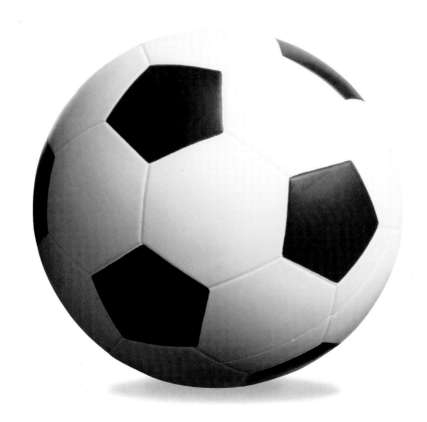

The button is a circle.

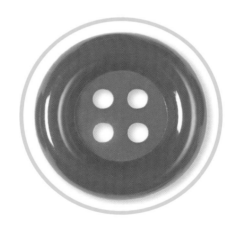